SUPER
SIMPLE
ORIGAMI

ORIGAMI
BIRDS

Easy & Fun Paper-Folding Projects

Anna George

Consulting Editor, Diane Craig, M.A./Reading Specialist

Super Sandcastle

An Imprint of Abdo Publishing
abdopublishing.com

abdopublishing.com

Published by Abdo Publishing, a division of ABDO, PO Box 398166, Minneapolis, Minnesota 55439.
Copyright © 2017 by Abdo Consulting Group, Inc. International copyrights reserved in all countries.
No part of this book may be reproduced in any form without written permission from the publisher.
Super SandCastle™ is a trademark and logo of Abdo Publishing.

Printed in the United States of America, North Mankato, Minnesota
102016
012017

**THIS BOOK CONTAINS
RECYCLED MATERIALS**

Editor: Liz Salzmann
Content Developer: Nancy Tuminelly
Cover and Interior Design and Production: Mighty Media, Inc.
Photo Credits: iStockphoto; Mighty Media, Inc.; Shutterstock
Special Thanks to Kazuko Collins

The following manufacturers/names appearing in this book are trademarks: Elmer's® Glue-All®

Publisher's Cataloging-in-Publication Data
Names: George, Anna, author.
Title: Origami birds: easy & fun paper-folding projects / by Anna George.
Other titles: Easy & fun paper-folding projects | Easy and fun paper-folding projects
Description: Minneapolis, MN : Abdo Publishing, 2017. | Series: Super simple origami
Identifiers: LCCN 2016944708 | ISBN 9781680784466 (lib. bdg.) |
    ISBN 9781680797992 (ebook)
Subjects: LCSH: Birds in art--Juvenile literature. | Origami--Juvenile literature.
    Paper work--Juvenile literature. | Handicraft--Juvenile literature.
Classification: DDC 736/.982--dc23
LC record available at http://lccn.loc.gov/2016944708

Super SandCastle™ books are created by a team of professional educators, reading specialists, and content developers around five essential components—phonemic awareness, phonics, vocabulary, text comprehension, and fluency—to assist young readers as they develop reading skills and strategies and increase their general knowledge. All books are written, reviewed, and leveled for guided reading and early reading intervention programs for use in shared, guided, and independent reading and writing activities to support a balanced approach to literacy instruction.

CONTENTS

AMAZING ORIGAMI BIRDS

Origami is the art of folding paper. In Japanese, the word *ori* means "to fold" and *gami* means "paper." People in Japan and all around the world enjoy origami.

Do you have a favorite bird? Is it an owl? Or maybe a swan? This book will show you how to make those birds and more! These super simple origami projects are great for beginners. You will learn about:

▶ different types of paper folds

▶ **symbols** used in origami **diagrams**

▶ types of paper that will work for origami

You'll be **amazed** at what you can make with just one sheet of paper!

BASIC FOLDS

MOUNTAIN FOLD
Fold behind to create a mountain.

VALLEY FOLD
Fold in front to create a valley.

CREASE
Fold and unfold to make a **crease**.

ORIGAMI SYMBOLS

The **symbols** below show the most common actions used in origami.

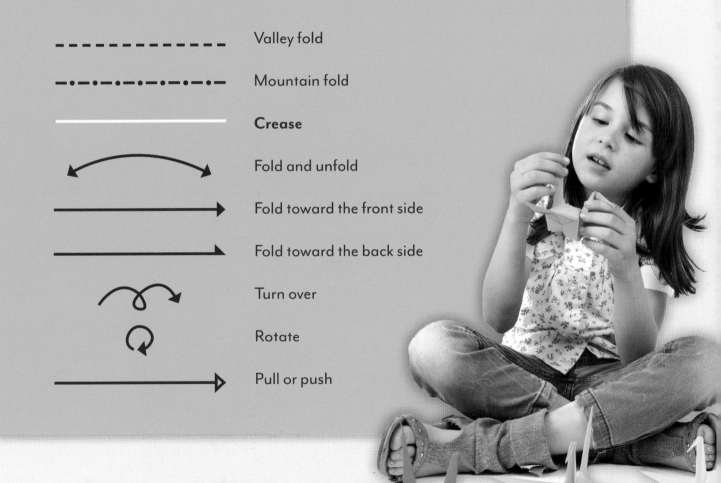

— — — — — — — — — — — —   Valley fold

—·—·—·—·—·—·—·—·—·—   Mountain fold

————————————   **Crease**

Fold and unfold

Fold toward the front side

Fold toward the back side

Turn over

Rotate

Pull or push

SPECIAL FOLDS

INSIDE REVERSE FOLD

This fold is often used to make the head or feet of an animal.
It may seem hard at first. After you practice it will become easier.
Here are instructions to make this fold.

1

Fold a square piece of
paper into a triangle. Valley
fold one of the points.

2

Crease it firmly.
Unfold.

3

Mountain fold the
crease. Unfold.

4

Unfold the paper. Place it so the
center crease is vertical. Valley
fold the bottom point.

5

Refold the
center crease.

OUTSIDE REVERSE FOLD

This fold is often used to make the head of a bird or the feet of an animal. It is just like the inside **reverse** fold except the corner is folded on the outside.

1

Fold a square piece of paper into a triangle. Valley fold one of the points.

2

Crease it firmly. Unfold.

3

Mountain fold the crease. Unfold.

4

Unfold the paper and turn it over. Place it so the center crease is vertical. Valley fold the bottom point.

5

Refold the center crease.

BASES

These shapes are used as bases for many different origami models. Practicing these will help you improve your origami.

SQUARE BASE

1
Place the paper on the table with a straight edge at the top. Mountain fold the top to the bottom. Unfold.

2
Mountain fold the right side to the left side. Unfold.

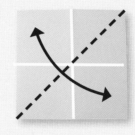

3
Valley fold one point to the opposite point. Unfold.

4
Valley fold the other two points together. Unfold.

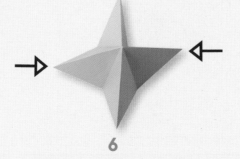

5
Pinch and lift two opposite mountain folds.

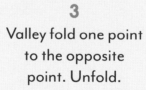

6
Press the sides together.

7
Flatten the paper into a square.

BIRD BASE

1

Start with a square base.
Place it with the open
point at the bottom.

2

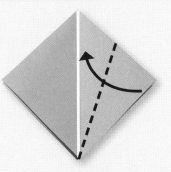

Valley fold the top
layer of the right point
to the center **crease**.

3

Valley fold the top
layer of the left point
to the center crease.

4

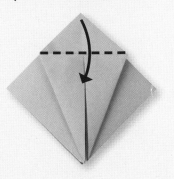

Valley fold the top point
down. Unfold the last
three folds you made.

5

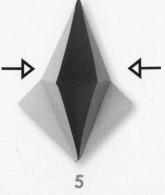

Lift the top layer of the
bottom point. Push the sides
together. Flatten the sides.

6

Turn the model over from
side to side. Repeat steps
2 through 5.

MATERIALS

BONE FOLDER

CRAFT STICK

PAPER

You can use almost any type of paper for origami. You can get special origami paper at craft stores or online. You can also use copy paper, magazine pages, scrapbooking paper, and even gift wrap!

CREASING TOOLS

The edge of a ruler, craft stick, or bone folder can help you make good **creases** and folds.

SCISSORS

You will need scissors if you are starting with a sheet of paper that isn't square. (See page 13.)

EXTRAS

These are **optional** supplies used in this book.

- googly eyes
- glue
- markers

ELMER'S
Glue-All
Multi-Purpose Glue

TIPS AND TRICKS

GET SQUARE

Many origami models use a square piece of paper.
It is easy to make a rectangular piece of paper square.

1 Fold one short edge so it lines up with a long edge.
   Crease the fold.

2 Cut off the strip under the triangle.

3 Unfold the paper. Now you have a square!

1

2

3

PRACTICE MAKES PERFECT!

When folding origami models, it is important for the folds to
be as **accurate** as possible. Match up the edges and corners
when folding. Make firm creases. The more folds there are,
the more important it is to make them exact. So get out some
scrap paper and practice, practice, practice!

FLAPPING BIRD

- paper (square)
- googly eyes
- glue

2

Valley fold the bottom point to the top point.

1

Place the paper on the table with a point at the top.

3

Valley fold the right point to form a narrow triangle.

4

Unfold the paper and turn it over. Pinch the sides of the small section together.

5

Hold the small section
and mountain fold
the center **crease**.

6

Rotate the model
so the center fold is
at the bottom.

7

The small triangle is
the bird's head. Glue
a googly eye to each
side of the head.

8

Hold the beak and the
tail. Pull gently to make
the wings flap!

WISE OLD OWL

- paper (square, different-colored sides)
- googly eyes
- glue

1
Place the paper on the table with a point at the top.

2
Valley fold the bottom point to the top point. Unfold.

3
Valley fold the other two points together. Unfold.

4
Valley fold the top point halfway to the center **crease**. Unfold.

5
Valley fold the top point to the small crease. Unfold.

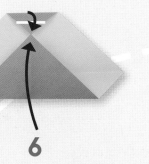

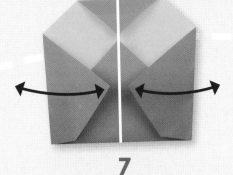

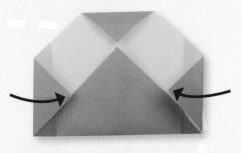

6

Valley fold the top point on the lower small **crease**. Valley fold the bottom corner up to meet the top corner.

7

Valley fold the side points to meet on the center crease. Unfold.

8

Valley fold the side points to line up with the sides of the bottom triangle.

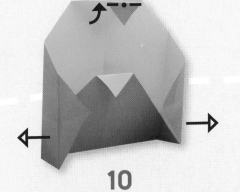

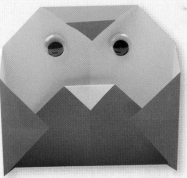

9

Valley fold the bottom center point down to form a beak.

10

Unfold the top point halfway so it sticks out. Mountain fold the tip of the point down. Pull the side flaps out to form rectangular sides. The owl should stand up.

11

Glue on the googly eyes.

SPINNING BIRD

- paper (square)
- googly eyes
- glue

1

Place the paper on the table with a point at the top. Your bird will be the color of the facedown side.

2

Valley fold the bottom point to the top point.

3

Valley fold the right point to the left point. Unfold.

4

Valley fold the top point below the bottom of the paper.

5

Valley fold the left point to the right point.

6

Rotate the model so the center **crease** is on the bottom. Valley fold the top layer as shown.

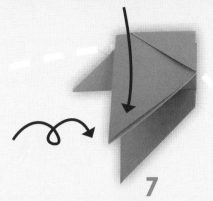

7

Turn the model over from side to side. Valley fold the other layer the same way. These are the wings.

8

The side point is the bird's head. Glue a googly eye to each side of the head.

9

Push the wings up. Toss the bird in the air and watch it spin!

PROPER PENGUIN

- paper (square, white and black)
- googly eyes
- glue

1

Place the paper on the table with a point at the top. The white side should face up.

2

Valley fold the right point to the left point. Unfold.

3

Valley fold the side points halfway to the center **crease**.

4

Valley fold the
top point to form
the head.

5

Turn the model
over from side to
side. Valley fold
the bottom point.

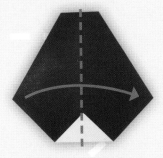

6

Valley fold the left point
to the right point.

7

Pull the beak out
slightly. Pinch
the back of the
head flat.

8

Glue a googly eye
to each side of
the head.

SWIMMING
SWAN
- paper (square)
- googly eyes
- glue

1

Place the paper on the table
with a point at the top.

2

Valley fold the right point to the
left point. Unfold.

3

Valley fold the bottom sides to the center **crease**.

4

Valley fold the sides to the center crease again.

5

Turn the model over from side to side.

Continued on the next page.

6

Valley fold the bottom point up to the top point.

7

Valley fold the left side to the right side. Rotate the model to the left.

8

Pull up on the point that is folded in the center. Pinch the right side to hold it at an angle. This is the swan's neck.

9

Valley fold the point down about halfway. Unfold.

10

Make an inside **reverse** fold on the **crease** (see page 8). This is the swan's head.

11

Spread the side folds slightly. This will help the swan stand upright.

12

Glue a googly eye to each side of the head.

FLYING BLUEBIRD

- paper (square)
- googly eyes
- glue

1

Place the paper on the table with a point at the top.

2

Valley fold the bottom point to the top point.

3

Valley fold the right point to the left point. Unfold.

26

4

Valley fold the top
corner down below the
lower edge of the paper.

5

Fold both layers of the
corner halfway back up.

6

Unfold the top
layer of the corner.

7

Valley fold the right point
to the left point. Rotate
the model to the left.

Continued
on the
next page.

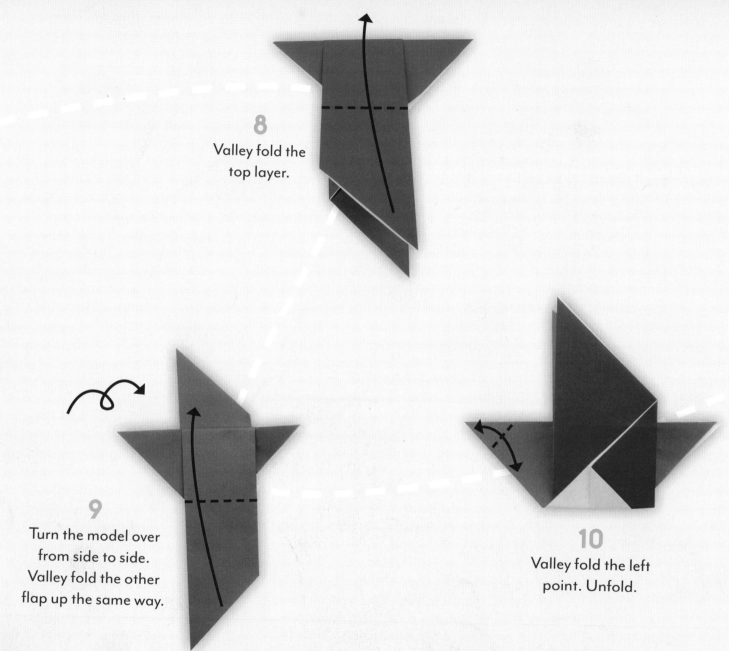

8

Valley fold the top layer.

9

Turn the model over from side to side. Valley fold the other flap up the same way.

10

Valley fold the left point. Unfold.

11

Make an inside **reverse** fold
on the **crease** (see page 8).
This is the bird's head.

12

Pull the beak out a bit.
Pinch the top of the
head to hold it in place.

13

Glue a googly eye to each
side of the head.

TRADITIONAL CRANE

· paper (square)

1

Start with a bird base.
(See pages 10 and 11.)
Place it with the divided
point at the bottom.

2

Valley fold the
top layer of the
right point to
the center.

3

Valley fold the top
layer of the left point
to the center.

4

Turn the model over from side to side. Repeat steps 2 and 3.

5

Valley fold both bottom points up. Unfold.

6

Make an outside **reverse** fold on each **crease** (see page 9). One point is the neck and the other is the tail.

7

Make an outside reverse fold on the tip of the neck. This forms the head.

8

Gently pull the wings apart.

GLOSSARY

accurate — exact or correct.

amaze — to surprise or fill with wonder.

crease — 1. a line made by folding something.
2. to make a sharp line in something by folding it.

diagram — a drawing that shows how something works or how parts go together.

optional — something you can choose, but is not required.

reverse — backwards, in the opposite direction.

symbol — an object or picture that stands for or represents something.